Kompetenzbereich: *Listening*

M1 On a New York double-decker bus tour

Have a look at the photos from New York.
Then listen once to what the tour guide says on the bus tour of Manhattan.
While listening, put the pictures (A–G) into the correct order (1–6).
There is one picture more than you need.

Stop number	1	2	3	4	5	6
Picture						

M2 Radio news

Listen to the radio news and tick (✓) the correct answer.
You will hear the recording only once.
You will have 15 seconds at the end of the recording to complete your answers.
You now have 30 seconds to look at the task.

1 What is the name of the radio station?

☐

☐

☐

☐

2 What is the time?

☐

☐

☐

☐

3 Where did the accident happen?

☐

☐

☐

☐

4 How many people were injured in the accident?

☐ 4 ☐ 3 ☐ 2 ☐ 1

5 What did the Prime Minister say?

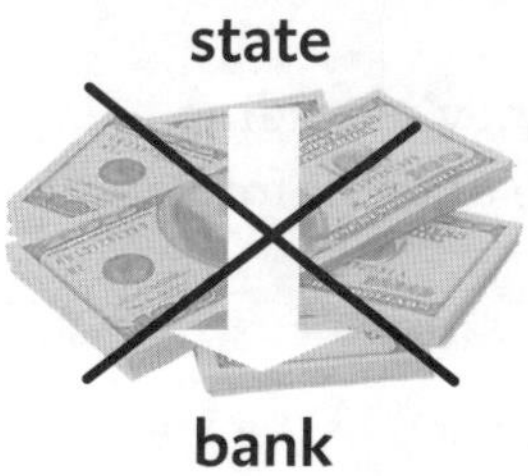

☐

☐

☐

☐

6 What did Barack Obama get?

☐

☐

☐

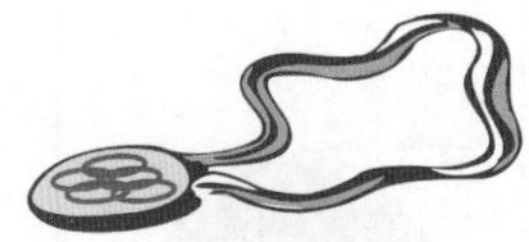

The Olympic Gold Medal in athletics

☐

7 Barack Obama grew up in …

☐

☐

☐

☐

8 What did Sue Barton win?

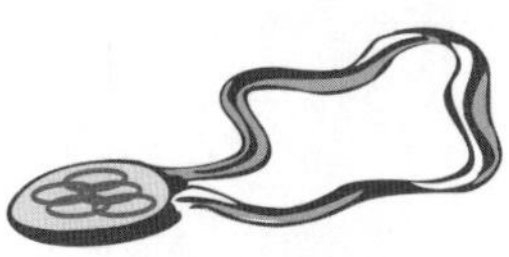

Gold Medal Olympic Games

☐

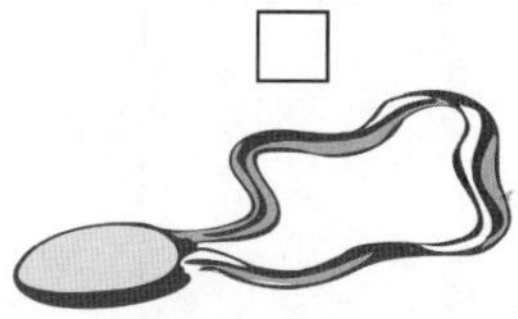

Gold Medal European Championships

☐

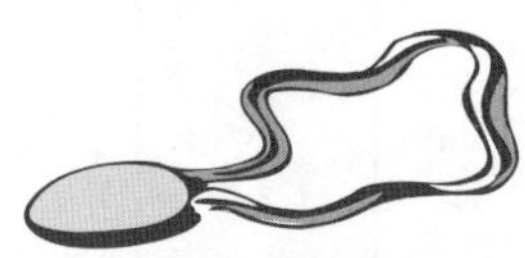

Gold Medal World Championships

☐

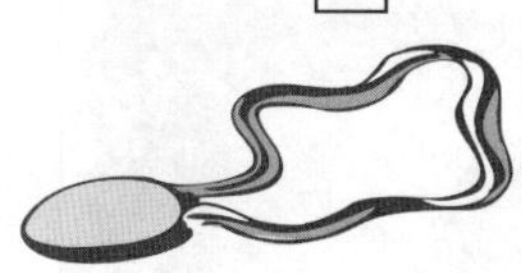

Gold Medal Australian Championships

☐

M3 Favourite books

Listen to the radio report. The reporter is asking three people about the books they're reading. While listening complete the table below in one or two words/numbers. Some of the information in the table has been completed for you.

You will hear the recording only <u>once</u>.

You will have 10 seconds at the end of the recording to complete your answers.

You now have 20 seconds to look at the task.

Person interviewed	Name	Age	Type of books they like reading	Name of the book they are reading at the moment
	Helen	____	____ stories	Murder ____
	____		biographies of ____ ____	
	____	____	____	Calvin and Hobbes

M4 A headmaster's announcement

Listen to a headmaster's announcement and tick (✓) the correct answer (a, b, c or d).
You will hear the recording only once.
You will have 10 seconds at the end of the recording to complete your answers.
You now have 40 seconds to look at the task.

1 What is the name of the school?

- a Greenwich Comprehensive School ☐
- b Ipswich Grammar School ☐
- c Ipswich Comprehensive School ☐
- d Greenwich Grammar School ☐

2 Until when will Mr Boyle not be selling any snacks or drinks?

- a Until Tuesday ☐
- b Until Wednesday ☐
- c Until Thursday ☐
- d Until Friday ☐

3 At what time will school finish tomorrow?

a ☐

b ☐

c ☐

d ☐

4 Where will the sports classes take place for the next two weeks if it's raining?

a

b

c

d

5 When will the theatre group perform their play?

- a Next Friday at 8 a.m. ☐
- b Next Saturday at 8 p.m. ☐
- c Next Friday at 8 p.m. ☐
- d Next Saturday at 8 a.m. ☐

M5 An American in Paris

Listen to the interview about a tourist in Paris and tick (✓) the correct answer (a, b, c or d).
You will hear the recording only <u>once</u>.
You will have 20 seconds at the end of the recording to complete your answers.
You now have 40 seconds to look at the task.

1 What magazine does the reporter work for?

- a The Travel Guide ☐
- b The Traveller ☐
- c The Time Traveller ☐
- d The Tourist ☐

2 Where is the tourist from?

- a Bosnia ☐
- b Baltimore ☐
- c Houston ☐
- d Boston ☐

3 Which of these Paris sights does the tourist not mention?

a

☐

b

☐

c

☐

d

☐

4 What does the tourist like about the French way of life (two things)?

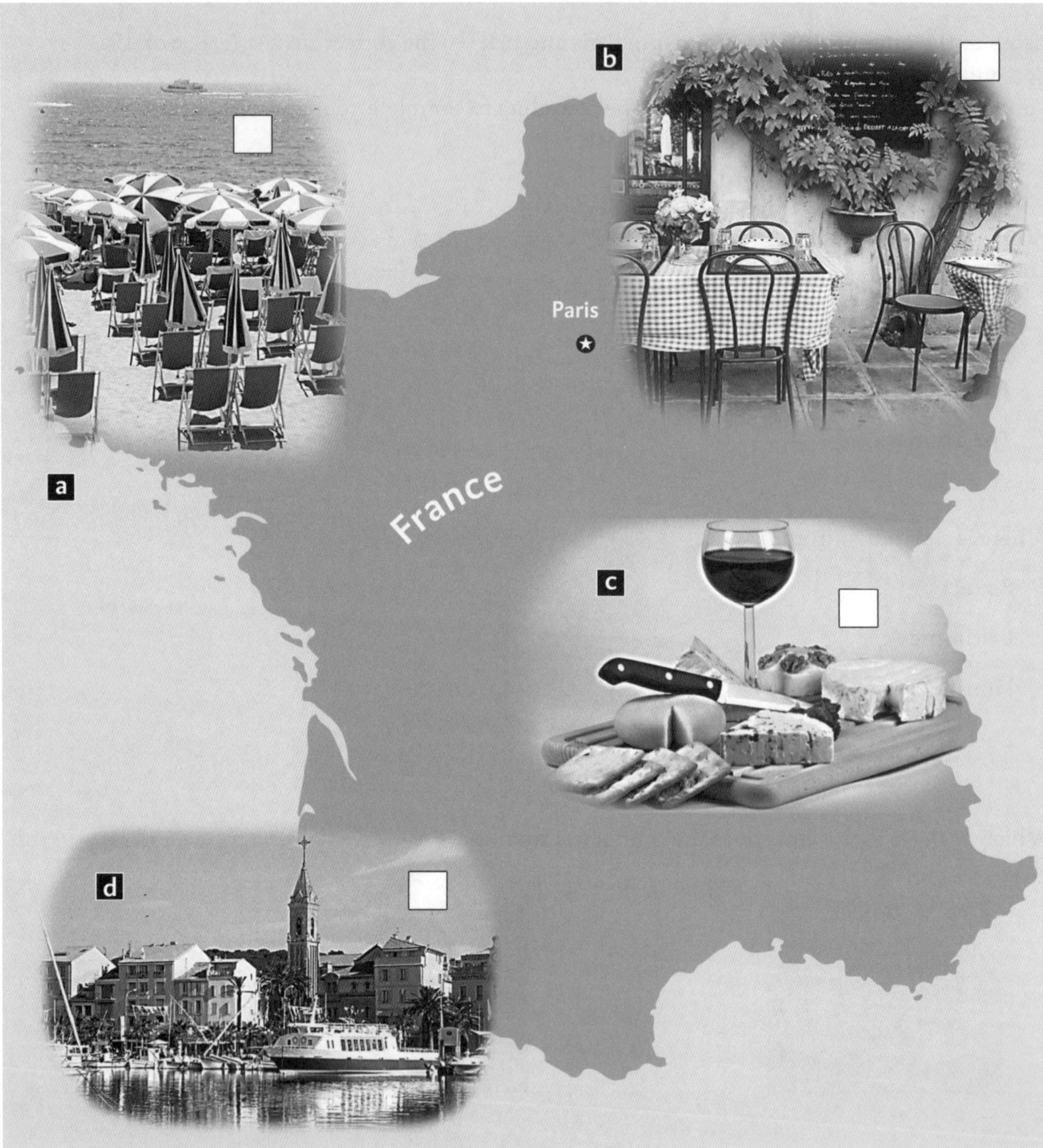

5 What is the only problem the tourist has?

- a The people aren't very friendly. ☐
- b He doesn't like the food. ☐
- c He has problems with the language. ☐
- d The hotel isn't very nice. ☐

M6 Message on the answering machine

Listen to the message on the answering machine.
While listening answer the following questions.
You will hear the recording only once.
You will have 20 seconds at the end of the recording to complete your answers.
You now have 20 seconds to look at the tasks.

1 Who is calling? ______________________

2 On what day is the barbecue? ______________________

3 Whose birthday is it? ______________________

4 What meat will they have? ______________________

5 What will the children get to drink? ______________________

6 When does the party start? ______________________

M7 Advertisements

You will hear two advertisements on the radio. Listen and complete the table below.
Decide if the information in the sentence is true or false and tick (✓) the right box.
You will hear the recording twice.
You will have 15 seconds at the end of the recording to complete your answers.
You now have 20 seconds to look at the tasks.

	true	false
1 The first advertisement is about a circus.	☐	☐
2 Ella is an old elephant.	☐	☐
3 There is a new restaurant at the zoo.	☐	☐
4 This Sunday a family ticket is only € 5.	☐	☐
5 You can get more information on the internet.	☐	☐
6 It is Rihanna's second concert in London.	☐	☐
7 There aren't any tickets left.	☐	☐
8 Two tickets cost £ 40.	☐	☐

Kompetenzbereich: *Reading*

M1 Youth hostel rules

Read the list of rules at a youth hostel (1 to 7). Then match them with one of the headlines (A to I). You won't need two of the headlines. Write your answers in the table at the end.

youth hostel rules

1 Guests with a reservation should arrive before 7 p.m. Otherwise the beds may be given to other visitors.

2 You can only stay at the hostel if you are a member of the Youth Hostel Association. You can join it at the hostel. Foreign visitors who aren't members of the Youth Hostel Association can buy an International Guest Card (Welcome Stamps).

3 Guests have to separate their rubbish and should be careful not to waste heating, water and electricity.

4 Anyone who has had too much to drink has to leave the hostel by order of the management.

5 In general, pets are not allowed in the hostel. Service and guide dogs for the blind, however, can be brought into the hostel.

6 The youth hostel is open until 10 p.m. Please be quiet from 10 p.m. to 7 a.m. in order not to disturb the night's sleep of the other guests.

7 On the day of your departure bedrooms must be vacated before 10 a.m.

A Conservation of nature and protection of our environment

B Leaving the hostel

C Rules at night

D Arrival time

E Animals in the hostel

F Smoking in the hostel

G Youth hostel membership

H Drinking alcohol

I Preparing meals

1	2	3	4	5	6	7

M2 An adventure holiday

Read the programm, then tick (✓) the correct answer (a, b, c or d).

Monday	7.00 p.m.	Arrival at **Carlingford Adventure Centre** Welcome & Programme
		Adventure Walk on Silver Mountain
	9.00 p.m.	Video/Board Games/Table Tennis/Volleyball
Tuesday	8.00 a.m.	Breakfast
	9.15 a.m.	Divide into groups of 8 and get ready
	9.30 a.m.	***Windsurfing/Kayaking/Water Skiing***
	1.00 p.m.	Lunch Optional Volleyball Session
	2.00 p.m.	***Rock climbing/Abseiling/Archery***
	6.00 p.m.	Dinner
	7.00 p.m.	Activity Session – ***Night in the forest***
	9.00 p.m.	Video/Board Games/Table Tennis/Volleyball
Wednesday	8.00 a.m.	Breakfast
	9.30 a.m.	***High Ropes*/Horse Riding/Low Ropes Course***
	1.00 p.m.	Lunch
	2.00 p.m.	***Sailing/Surfing/Canoeing***
	5.00 p.m.	Departure

* *Suitable for children aged 14 years and older*

1 When will the guests arrive at the adventure centre?

a Monday morning ☐

b Monday evening ☐

c Tuesday evening ☐

d Wednesday morning ☐

2 On what day do they offer water sports in the afternoon?

- **a** Monday ☐
- **b** Tuesday ☐
- **c** Wednesday ☐
- **d** never ☐

3 What do they offer on Tuesday after lunch until 2 p.m.?

- **a** rock climbing ☐
- **b** surfing ☐
- **c** sailing ☐
- **d** volleyball ☐

4 How old should you be for the High Ropes?

- **a** Your age doesn't matter. ☐
- **b** under 14 years of age ☐
- **c** not older than 14 years ☐
- **d** 14 years or older ☐

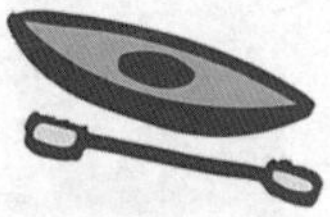

5 On Tuesday morning they will form groups for the activities. There should be …

- **a** 8 people in one group. ☐
- **b** 8 groups. ☐
- **c** a meeting of the groups at 8 o'clock. ☐
- **d** 2 groups. ☐

6 When can you play table tennis?

- **a** after 9 o'clock in the morning ☐
- **b** after 9 o'clock in the evening ☐
- **c** until 9 o'clock in the evening ☐
- **d** They don't offer table tennis. ☐

M3 The football world cup

Read the text. Then match each statement (1 to 7) with one of the photos (a to h).
There is one more photo than you need.
Write your answers in the table at the end.

1 A fan in the stadium is cheering for her team.

2 A fan is holding up a banner.

3 A man with a funny hat is praying for his team to win.

4 A boy is sitting on the grass watching a football match.

5 A fan with a painted face is looking serious.

6 A player is getting ready for a corner kick.

7 A black and a white football fan are having fun together.

a

b
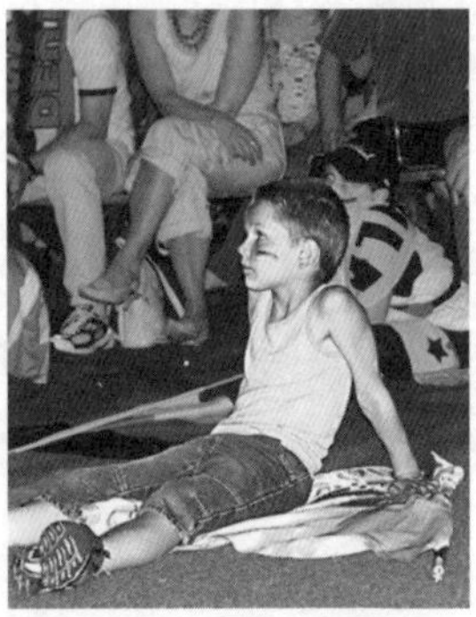

c

d

e

f

g

h

1	2	3	4	5	6	7

M4 Advice for teenagers

Read the text. Then decide if the statements are true, false or not given in the text.
Tick (✓) the correct box.

Post Reply | Page 1 of 3 | 1 2 3

Thread Tools | Display Modes

16.08 15.15

Toby95

Member

Problem: Parent trouble
My parents don't understand me. If I want to talk to them, they don't want to hear what I have to say. I really want them to understand me and be there for me, but they always decide things without asking me.
They always say this or that is the best for me.
They drive me crazy! It's so frustrating!

Quote

16.08 17.48

Lisa McEwan

Teen Forum Advisor

☆☆☆☆☆

Answer: As a teen, it's normal for you to feel that your parents don't take you seriously. Some day, when you're older, you and your parents will get on much better. But this is the best you can do now:

1. When you and your parents have different opinions, talk about them in a calm and respectful way.
2. Don't argue about every little thing with your parents. Save your energy for important things. In fact, often you'll be a lot happier if you just cool down and walk away.
3. Always remember: Your parents still love you and it would really hurt them, if anything bad happened to you. Seriously. Sometimes you think that isn't true, but deep down you know it is.
4. Keep in mind whenever your parents are stressing you out: In a few years you'll be 18 and you'll be able to make important decisions for yourself. Just be patient.

Quote

		true	false	not given
1	This text is about a boy and his school problems.	☐	☐	☐
2	The boy's parents don't understand him.	☐	☐	☐
3	The boy's parents are divorced.	☐	☐	☐
4	His parents always ask him before they make decisions.	☐	☐	☐
5	Advice 1 says that you should stay calm when arguing with your parents.	☐	☐	☐
6	Advice 2 says that arguing with your parents gives you a lot of energy.	☐	☐	☐
7	Advice 3 says that your parents don't want anything bad happen to you.	☐	☐	☐
8	Advice 4 says that in a few years a lot will have changed.	☐	☐	☐

M5 Fairyland Magic Ticket

Read the text. Then answer the questions in 1 to 5 words/numbers.

1 How many days is the Magic Ticket valid for?

2 Within what period of time can you use the Magic Ticket for one day?

3 How many parks can you use the ticket for?

4 How much can you save with this special ticket?

5 Until what date can you get a Magic Ticket for that price?

6 How much does a 13-year old boy have to pay for a Magic Ticket?

7 How much is a Magic Ticket for a 3-year old girl?

M6 Miley Cyrus

Read the text. Then complete the table on the next page in 1 to 5 words/numbers.

Miley Ray Cyrus was born as Destiny Hope Cyrus on 23th November 1992, in Nashville, Tennessee. She is a singer and songwriter. Miley became famous for her role as Miley Stewart on the television series *Hannah Montana.*

Miley's parents are Billy Ray Cyrus and Leticia "Tish" Cyrus. When Miley was born, she was named "Destiny Hope" because her parents thought she would have big success in life. Soon, however, they started to call her "Smiley" – later shortened to "Miley" – because she always smiled as a baby.

Miley Cyrus has a little sister named Noah and a little brother named Braison. Billy Ray and Tish also have children from previous relationships: Billy Ray adopted Tish's children Trace and Brandi when they were very young. Billy Ray's son Christopher Cody is Miley's half-brother.

to audition: vorsprechen

When she was eleven years old, Miley auditioned for the television series *Hannah Montana. Hannah Montana* is a show about a girl named Miley Stewart who is also a singer, but only her family and friends know this. The president of Disney Channel said that Miley was given the role because she was so lively and full of energy. She seemed to be a person who loves every minute of her life.

charity: Wohlfahrtsorganisation

As the star of *Hannah Montana*, Miley became popular with children and teenagers, leading to a successful career in music. In 2007, Miley earned about $ 18.2 million. She celebrated her 16th birthday at Disneyland, which was closed for the event. 5 000 fans came to the party and paid $ 250 per ticket. The money was given to the charity Youth Service America, a youth volunteering organization.

In the future Miley Cyrus wants to concentrate on her career as an actress and take a break from the music industry.

WANTED

Name Miley Cyrus

1. Date of birth ____________________

2. Nickname as a baby ____________________

3. Miley's younger brothers and sisters ____________________

4. Name of the character she plays in "Hannah Montana" ____________________

5. Income in 2007 ____________________

6. Price of ticket for Miley's birthday party ____________________

7. Name of the organisation that got the money raised at her party ____________________

____

____

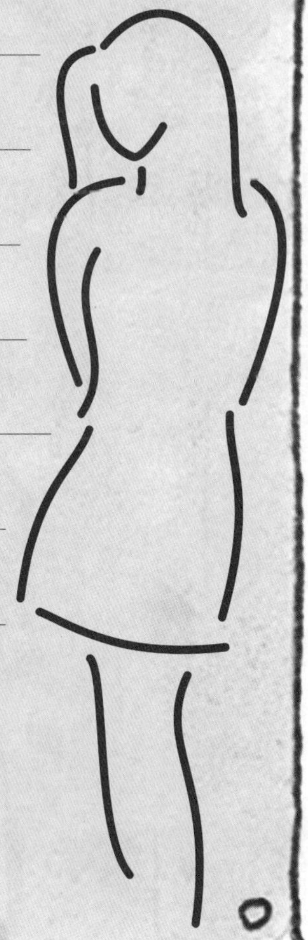

M 7 A fancy dress party

Read the text. Then answer the questions below using 1 to 7 words/numbers.

1 When is the party?

a day of the week: ______________________

b date: ______________________

2 On what special day does the party take place?

____

3 When does it begin and finish?

a start: ______________________

b end: ______________________

4 Who can go to the party?

____

5 How much do the tickets cost?

____

6 Where can you buy the tickets?

____

7 Where is the party?

____

8 What kind of clothes should you wear?

____

____

Kompetenzbereich: *Language in use*

M 1 Comparisons

Jack and Jim are talking about football. Tick (✓) the correct solution of the three possibilities.

JIM: What's your ☐ favour ☐ favouritest ☐ favourite football team?

JACK: I think Manchester United is ☐ best ☐ the better ☐ the best team in the world.

JIM: But isn't Bayern Munich ☐ as good as ☐ as good than ☐ as better as Manchester United?

JACK: I think Manchester United are even better ☐ as ☐ than ☐ else Bayern Munich

because they have the ☐ expensivest ☐ more expensive ☐ most expensive players of all European teams.

JIM: But that doesn't always mean that they are better.

Sometimes a young talented player is ☐ cheap ☐ more cheap ☐ cheaper than an older player and just as good.

M2 Conversation

Imagine that you are spending two weeks at your pen friend's house in England. Daniel, your pen friend, is talking to you about free time activities. What would you say in English?

1 DU: Frage, was ihr heute Abend machen könnt.

---

2 DANIEL: Do you play football or rugby?
DU: *Sage, dass du Fußball gerne magst, aber noch nie Rugby gespielt hast.*

---

3 DANIEL: I play in our local rugby team and tonight I have to go to training.
DU: *Frage, ob du mitkommen kannst.*

---

4 DANIEL: Of course you can and I can show you how to play rugby.
DU: *Frage, ob Rugby gefährlicher ist als Fußball.*

---

5 DANIEL: No, it's not. Do you play football at home in Germany?
DU: *Sage, dass du nicht in einer Mannschaft spielst, aber dass du oft mit deinen Freunden spielst, einfach zum Spaß.*

---

6 DANIEL: Have you ever watched a big football match live?
DU: *Sage, dass du letztes Jahr das Spiel zwischen Werder Bremen und Manchester United gesehen hast.*

---

7 DANIEL: Wow, I would have liked to see that! I'm a big fan of Manchester United.
DU: *Sage, dass es sogar deiner Schwester gefallen hat und sie interessiert sich nicht für Fußball.*

---

8 DANIEL: So she's just like my sister.
DU: *Frage Daniel, was seine Schwester mag.*

DANIEL: She loves buying new clothes, but that is a very expensive hobby, of course.

M3 Prepositions

Look at the photograph and then complete each sentence with the right preposition from the box.
Don't use any of the prepositions twice.
There are more prepositions in the box than you need.

at – beside – for – along – between – of – on – on top of – across – before – in – behind – about

1 The picture shows a family ______________ the child's bedroom.

2 They are looking ______________ some photographs on the carpet.

3 The child is sitting ______________ the parents.

4 The Dad hasn't got any shoes ______________.

5 The child's bed is ______________ the parents.

6 There's a chest of drawers on the left and there are two photos ______________ the chest of drawers.

7 There is a basket for a baby ______________ the bed.

8 Maybe the basket is ______________ the family's new baby that will be born soon.

M4 Signs

What is the meaning of the following signs?
There are always <u>two</u> correct answers.

1

- a Only bicycles may go this way. ☐
- b Only bicycles won't go this way. ☐
- c Only bicycles are allowed to go this way. ☐
- d Only bicycles shouldn't go this way. ☐

2

- a You needn't smoke here. ☐
- b You don't have to smoke here. ☐
- c You can't smoke here. ☐
- d You mustn't smoke here. ☐

3

- a You need to wear a helmet. ☐
- b You could wear a helmet. ☐
- c You have to wear a helmet. ☐
- d You would wear a helmet. ☐

4

- a Animals should cross the road. ☐
- b Animals might cross the road. ☐
- c Animals must cross the road. ☐
- d Animals can cross the road. ☐

5

- a You must turn off your mobile phone. ☐
- b You would like to turn off your mobile phone. ☐
- c You have to turn off your mobile phone. ☐
- d You can turn off your mobile phone. ☐

6

- a You don't have to go 30 mph or slower anymore. ☐
- b You mustn't go 30 mph or slower anymore. ☐
- c You don't want to go 30 mph or slower anymore. ☐
- d You don't need to go 30 mph or slower anymore. ☐

M5 Verb phrases

Sally and Tina, two teenagers, meet on the bus.
Fill in the missing prepositions.
Choose them from the box:

(look) after/for/at	(get) up/off /on	(give) up/in/out

SALLY: Hi, Tina. Where are you going?

TINA: I have to baby-sit for my aunt, I have to look ______________ her two-year old daughter. She's asleep in bed and there's not much for me to do but my aunt wants me to be there if the child wants to get ______________.

SALLY: Where do you have to get ______________ the bus?

TINA: I don't know. Let's look ______________ the map over there.

SALLY: What's the name of the street that you're looking ______________?

TINA: Shop Street. But I can't find it on the map. Can you find it?

SALLY: No, I can't. You better give ______________ and ask the bus driver.

TINA: Good idea!

M6 Mixed grammar and vocabulary exercise

Read the text about a teenager's family.
Tick (✓) the correct solution from the three possibilities or write down the right word(s) on the lines below the pictures.

Tom is talking to his friend on the phone:

Sometimes my parents can
☐ are
☐ be
☐ is
unfair!

My parents love my little sister more
☐ as
☐ else
☐ than
me.

She always
☐ became
☐ becomes
☐ gets
what she
☐ wants.
☐ wills.
☐ will.

But as soon as she has something she
☐ wants it not
☐ will it not
☐ doesn't want it
anymore.

☐ For ten minutes
☐ Ten minutes ago
☐ Ten minutes long
she suddenly came into the

______________________________.

I was watching a film on TV there.

She
☐ didn't like that
☐ didn't liked
☐ liked that not
and
☐ says
☐ is saying
☐ said
to my parents:

"I
- ☐ will that no watch!
- ☐ like not to watch that!
- ☐ don't want to watch that!

Can I watch something
- ☐ more?"
- ☐ else?"
- ☐ other?"

I said:

"There isn't
- ☐ anything
- ☐ nothing
- ☐ something

nice on TV for small

______________________________."

"But we have
- ☐ much
- ☐ lots of
- ☐ a little

nice DVDs for kids", she said and began to cry.

So of course my parents helped her and now she
- ☐ is watching
- ☐ watching
- ☐ is watch

her stupid film.

That's so unfair!

But tomorrow I will go

____

with my Dad – just the two of us.

Kompetenzbereich: *Writing*

M1 My favourite star

Read the poster below about a writing competition in STAR MAGAZINE.

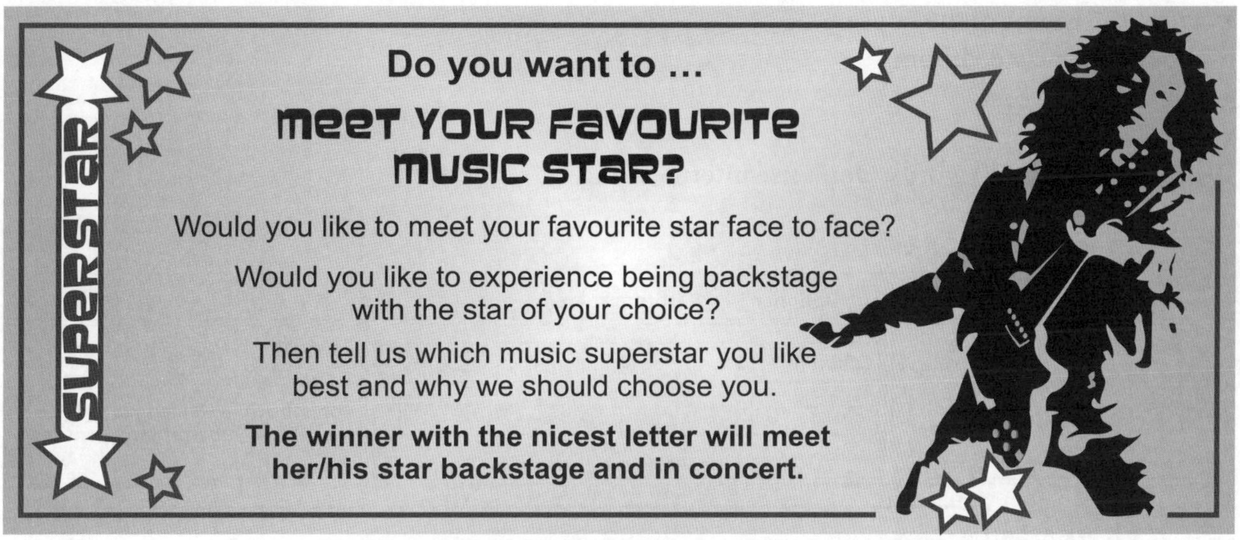

Write a letter to Mrs Susan Lenihan, the editor of STAR MAGAZINE, telling her …

- about your favourite music star (age, where she/he lives, music style).
- why you like her/him best.
- what CDs, posters, T-shirts, etc. you have.
- what you think it would be like to meet your star.

Write 80 to 100 words.

M2 Our new house

You and your family have just moved to a new house and you really like it.
Write an email to your English pen-friend Jim about your new home.

Tell him …

- what the house looks like.
- about the rooms of the house.
- about your new bedroom.
- what you like best.
- …

Write about 60 to 80 words. Don't use internet slang.

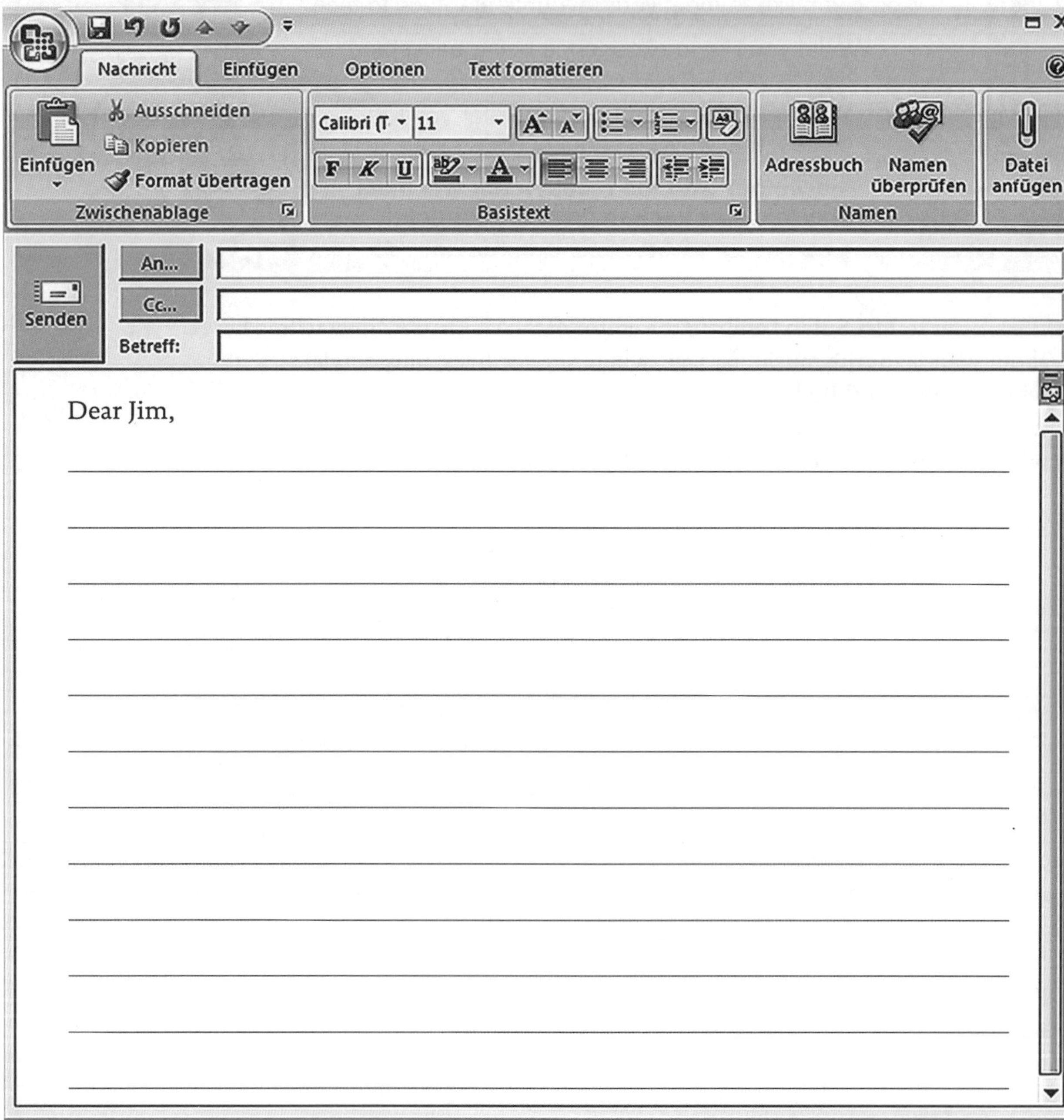

M3 The lost pencil case

You have lost your pencil case at school and you put a notice on the board with a description of the pencil case. Here is how it looks like:
Write about 30–50 words.

Hi there,

Last Monday I lost my pencil case at school. This is what it looks like:

____

____

____

____

____

____

____

____

If you find it please call John at
963 54 72 64 22

M4 A note

You are staying with the Johnson family in Florida and you have just hurt your foot. Now you want to go to the doctor to get it seen to. The Johnsons are not at home at the moment so you leave them a note.

In this note you tell them …

- where you are.
- why you went there.
- how you hurt your foot.
- when you will be back.

Write about 40 to 50 words.

Best.-Nr. 9355002

M 4 A note

Lösungsvorschlag:

Dear Mr. and Mrs. Johnson,

I have gone to the doctor's because I hurt my foot playing soccer in the garden. I should be back for dinner at 7 p.m. as I don't think that it's anything serious.

See you later,

Robert

Kompetenzbereich: *Listening*

M 1 On a New York double-decker bus tour

Welcome to the New York Double Decker Bus Tour! We'll start our tour here at Times Square in downtown Manhattan. Now we're turning into Broadway and you can see huge advertisements of musicals on the façades of the buildings.

The highest skyscraper in New York at present is the Empire State Building with its 102 floors. In the movie "King Kong" a gigantic gorilla was standing on top of the building fighting airplanes.

One of New York's first skyscrapers was the famous Flatiron Building. It has a very funny triangular shape and two of the best known streets in New York – 5th Avenue and Broadway – meet at one of the three corners of the building.

The Rockefeller Center is a very popular place to go ice-skating in winter and every Christmas they put up a huge Christmas tree here.

Here you see the United Nations Headquarters. The sculpture in front of the building is called the "Knotted Gun" and is a symbol of hope for peace and less violence in the world.

This park is called Central Park and over there on the ground you can see a mosaic in the shape of a circle. This is called Strawberry Fields and was made in memory of John Lennon, who was a member of the famous band "The Beatles".

This is the end of the tour. I wish you a pleasant stay in New York!

Stop number	1	2	3	4	5	6
Picture	G	F	C	A	E	B

M2 Radio news

This is Radio 2FM. You're listening to the news at 4 pm. These are the headlines for today:

London. Serious car accident on the A52 between Derby and Nottingham. A young driver fell asleep at the wheel and collided with an oncoming car carrying four people. The young driver was killed instantly and three of the passengers in the other car are seriously injured in a Nottingham hospital. The driver of the second car escaped with minor injuries.

London. This morning the Prime Minister announced that the state is not going to help the West Midlands Bank, which is facing serious financial problems. He said: "The state won't give any money to the bank."

Oslo. This year's Nobel Peace Prize will go to US-President Barack Obama. Mr Obama grew up in Hawaii, but for several years of his childhood he also lived in Indonesia with his family. He later went to Columbia University in New York and graduated from Harvard Law School. In 2009 he took office as the 44th President of the United States.

Sports: Sydney. Sheffield athlete Sue Barton won the gold medal in the 400 metre hurdles at the World Championships in Melbourne, Australia. This is her first gold at a World Championships.

And now the weather forecast for the next few days …

1 What is the name of the radio station?

☐

☑

☐

☐

2 What is the time?

☑

☐

☐

☐

3 Where did the accident happen?

☐

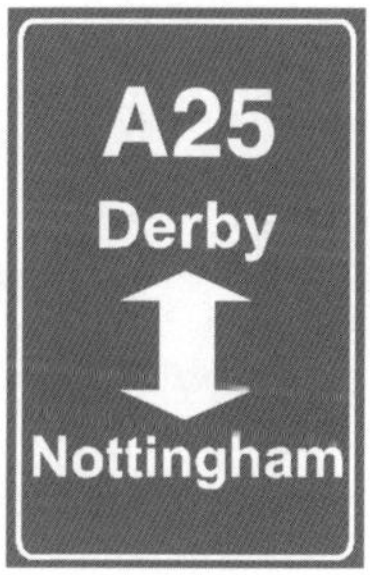

☐

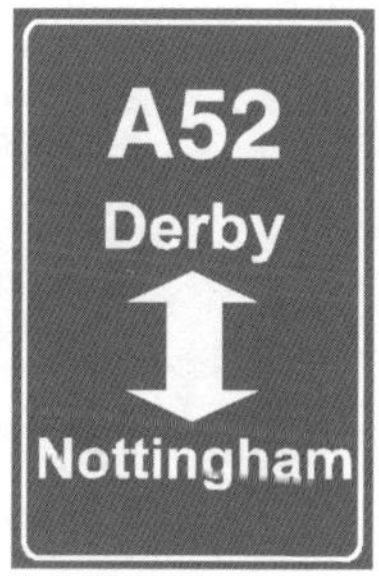

☑

☐

4 How many people were injured in the accident?

☑ 4 ☐ 3 ☐ 2 ☐ 1

5 What did the Prime Minister say?

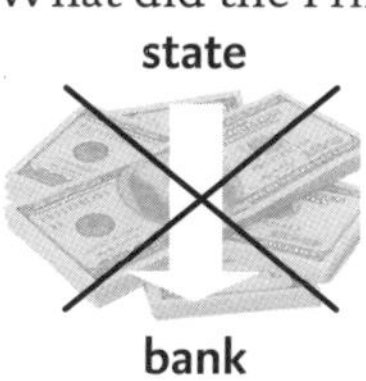

☑

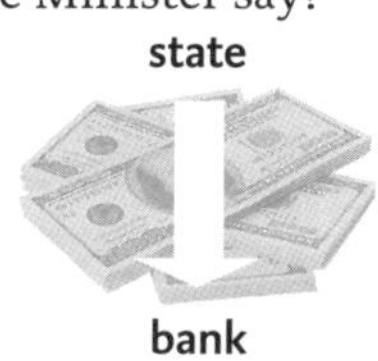

☐

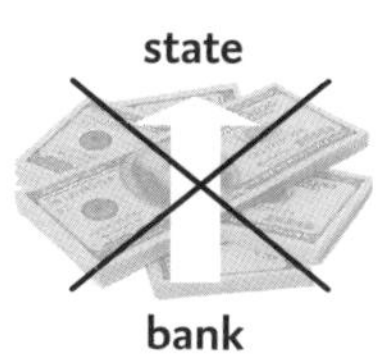

☐

☐

6 What did Barack Obama get?

☐

☑

☐

The Olympic Gold Medal in athletics

☐

7 Barack Obama grew up in …

☐

☑

☐

☐

8 What did Sue Barton win?

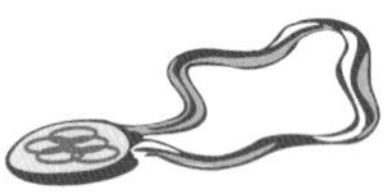

Gold Medal
Olympic Games

☐

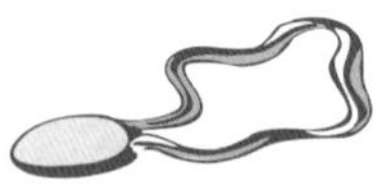

Gold Medal
European Championships

☐

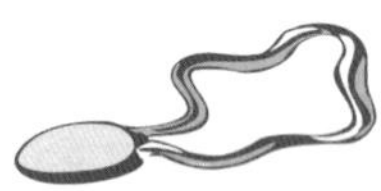

Gold Medal
World Championships

☑

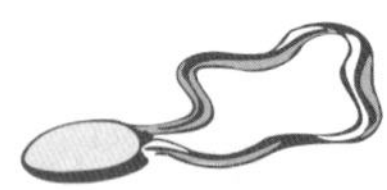

Gold Medal
Australian Championships

☐

M3 Favourite books

REPORTER: Dear listeners, we're here in Shop Street in Brighton on a lovely Saturday morning – and this week we're asking people in the street: What book are you reading at the moment?

HELEN: Hello. I'm Helen and I'm 38 years old. I've just finished an exciting crime story called "Murder at work". I just couldn't stop reading and I had no idea who the murderer was until I read the very last page.

DAVE: Hi, I'm Dave. I'm Helen's husband. Well, I'm not reading a book at the moment, but I like reading biographies of famous people and their interesting lives.

SALLY: Hi, I'm Sally. I'm Dave and Helen's daughter and I'm 12 years old. What I really like reading are comics. I even have one here in my bag, it's called "Calvin and Hobbes". I love the funny stories with the boy and his tiger. They're so funny.

Person interviewed	Name	Age	Type of books they like reading	Name of the book they are reading at the moment
	Helen	38	crime stories	Murder at work
	Dave		biographies of famous people	
	Sally	12	comics	Calvin and Hobbes

M4 A headmaster's announcement

[signal]

Good morning boys and girls,

first of all, I'd like to wish you all the best for the new school year here at Ipswich Comprehensive School.

I have four important announcements for you:

Mr Boyle won't be selling any snacks or drinks until Thursday, so please make sure that you bring whatever you need with you until then.

School will finish at 2.30 p.m. tomorrow because of an important teachers' meeting in the afternoon.

The renovation of our gym isn't quite finished, so for this week and next week sports lessons will take place on the football grounds or – if it's raining – in the assembly hall.

Due to great demand our theatre group will hold a repeat performance of the play "Don't Hold your Breath" next Friday at 8 p.m.

1 What is the name of the school?

- a Greenwich Comprehensive School ☐
- b Ipswich Grammar School ☐
- c Ipswich Comprehensive School ☑
- d Greenwich Grammar School ☐

2 Until when will Mr Boyle not be selling any snacks or drinks?

- a Until Tuesday ☐
- b Until Wednesday ☐
- c Until Thursday ☑
- d Until Friday ☐

3 At what time will school finish tomorrow?

a 

☐

b 

☑

c 

☐

d 

☐

4 Where will the sports classes take place for the next two weeks if it's raining?

- a "Sports classes on the football grounds" ☐
- b "Sports classes in the assembly hall" ☐
- c "Sports classes in the gym" ☑
- d "There won't be any sports lessons in the next two weeks." ☐

5 When will the theatre group perform their play?

- a Next Friday at 8 a.m. ☐
- b Next Saturday at 8 p.m. ☐
- c Next Friday at 8 p.m. ☑
- d Next Saturday at 8 a.m. ☐

M5 An American in Paris

REPORTER: Hello. I'm from the British magazine "The Traveller" and I'd like to talk to you about your stay here in Paris. How are you enjoying yourself?

TOURIST: Oh, very much. Paris is wonderful.

REPORTER: Where are you from?

TOURIST: I'm from Boston, USA. I've always wanted to come to Europe and especially Paris, but it's even more beautiful than I thought it would be.

REPORTER: Have you done any sightseeing yet?

TOURIST: Oh, yes. First of all I climbed up the Eiffel Tower. The view from up there is spectacular! Then I went to the great museum called the "Louvre" to see Mona Lisa smiling. I was amazed at the amount of fabulous paintings and other works of art there. But what I liked best was the huge castle outside Paris, the palace of the "sun king".

REPORTER: Oh, you mean Versailles?

TOURIST: That's it.

REPORTER: And what do you think about the French way of life?

TOURIST: I just love it! They have wonderful markets with delicious cheese and wine and the cafés are great, too. It's all so different to what we are used to back home in the States. The only problem is that my French isn't very good and not many people here speak English, but I'm managing fine.

REPORTER: Thank you very much for taking the time to talk to me.

1 What magazine does the reporter work for?

- a The Travel Guide ☐
- b The Traveller ☑
- c The Time Traveller ☐
- d The Tourist ☐

2 Where is the tourist from?

a Bosnia ☐

b Baltimore ☐

c Houston ☐

d Boston ☑

3 Which of these Paris sights does the tourist not mention?

a  ☐

b  ☐

c  ☑

d  ☐

4 What does the tourist like about the French way of life (two things)?

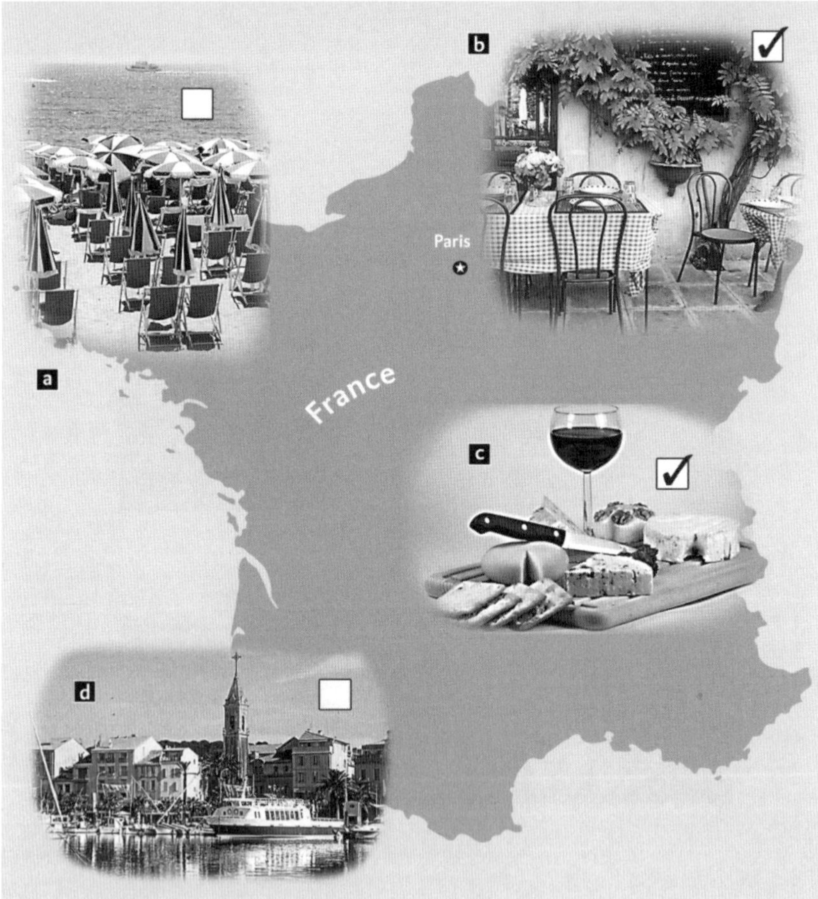

5 What is the only problem the tourist has?

- a The people aren't very friendly. ☐
- b He doesn't like the food. ☐
- c He has problems with the language. ☑
- d The hotel isn't very nice. ☐

M6 Message on the answering machine

Hi Tom, this is John. Sorry to have missed you. The reason I'm calling is to invite you to a barbecue next Saturday at our house. We are celebrating Ann's 30th birthday and we decided to have a barbecue because the weather will be very nice next weekend. Of course all the family is invited. You don't need to bring anything. Food and drinks will be provided. We will have steaks and potatoes and a selection of salads and breads. Wine and beer will be available for the adults and lemonade for the children. The party starts at 5 p.m., but it's no problem if you come later. We hope you'll be able to make it. Please let us know. Talk to you soon. Goodbye.

1 John

2 (next) Saturday

3 Ann('s)

4 steaks

5 lemonade

6 5 p.m.

M7 Advertisements

Advertisement 1:

Enjoy a nice family day out at Dublin Zoo where fabulous fun is guaranteed for the whole family. Meet the new baby elephant Ella or go to see the two-week-old polar bear Snowy. At Dublin Zoo there is something for everyone to see. And why not savour a meal at our fabulous new restaurant, which serves a variety of homemade foods or sample a delicious scone with homemade jam and clotted cream at our café. The zoo boasts two playgrounds catering to the needs of all age groups. Pony rides are also available for just € 2. Take advantage of the reduced rates this Sunday. Single tickets cost just € 5 saving you € 2 and a family ticket costs € 10 saving you € 5. Click on www.dublinzoo.ie for more information. Our friendly staff look forward to making you feel welcome at Ireland's best zoo.

Advertisement 2:

Don't miss a fabulous night out with your friends at London's Concert Hall this weekend. Rihanna is appearing in concert for the first time ever in London. It's an event not to be missed. Tickets are still available. Just call 01637890021 or purchase your tickets online. Just click on www.london-tickets.co.uk. But don't wait too long or you might just miss the night of a lifetime. Tickets cost just £ 40.

		true	false
1	The first advertisement is about a circus.	☐	☑
2	Ella is an old elephant.	☐	☑
3	There is a new restaurant at the zoo.	☑	☐
4	This Sunday a family ticket is only € 5.	☐	☑
5	You can get more information on the internet.	☑	☐
6	It is Rihanna's second concert in London.	☐	☑
7	There aren't any tickets left.	☐	☑
8	Two tickets cost £ 40.	☐	☑

Kompetenzbereich: *Reading*

M 1 Youth hostel rules

1	2	3	4	5	6	7
D	G	A	H	E	C	B

M 2 An adventure holiday

1 When will the guests arrive at the adventure centre?

- a Monday morning ☐
- b Monday evening ☑
- c Tuesday evening ☐
- d Wednesday morning ☐

2 On what day do they offer water sports in the afternoon?

- a Monday ☐
- b Tuesday ☐
- c Wednesday ☑
- d never ☐

3 What do they offer on Tuesday after lunch until 2 p.m.?

- a rock climbing ☐
- b surfing ☐
- c sailing ☐
- d volleyball ☑

4 How old should you be for the High Ropes?

- a Your age doesn't matter. ☐
- b under 14 years of age ☐
- c not older than 14 years ☐
- d 14 years or older ☑

5 On Tuesday morning they will form groups for the activities. There should be …

- a 8 people in one group. ☑
- b 8 groups. ☐
- c a meeting of the groups at 8 o'clock. ☐
- d 2 groups. ☐

6 When can you play table tennis?

- a after 9 o'clock in the morning ☐
- b after 9 o'clock in the evening ☑
- c until 9 o'clock in the evening ☐
- d They don't offer table tennis. ☐

M3 The football world cup

1	2	3	4	5	6	7
d	f	c	b	e	a	h

M 4 Advice for teenagers

		true	false	not given
1	This text is about a boy and his school problems.	☐	☑	☐
2	The boy's parents don't understand him.	☑	☐	☐
3	The boy's parents are divorced.	☐	☐	☑
4	His parents always ask him before they make decisions.	☐	☑	☐
5	Advice 1 says that you should stay calm when arguing with your parents.	☑	☐	☐
6	Advice 2 says that arguing with your parents gives you a lot of energy.	☐	☑	☐
7	Advice 3 says that your parents don't want anything bad happen to you.	☑	☐	☐
8	Advice 4 says that in a few years a lot will have changed.	☑	☐	☐

M 5 Fairyland Magic Ticket

1 1

2 6 months

3 2

4 15 %

5 12th November 2010

6 £ 51.00

7 £ 44.00

M6 Miley Cyrus

WANTED

Name	*Miley Cyrus*
1. Date of birth	*23th November 1992*
2. Nickname as a baby	*Smiley*
3. Miley's younger brothers and sisters	*Noah and Braison*
4. Name of the character she plays in "Hannah Montana"	*Miley Stewart*
5. Income in 2007	*$ 18.2 million*
6. Price of ticket for Miley's birthday party	*$ 250*
7. Name of the organisation that got the money raised at her party	*Youth Service America*

M7 A fancy dress party

1 a Saturday

b 14 July

2 the last day of the school year

3 a 7 p.m.

b 10 p.m.

4 classes 8 and 9

5 £2

6 in the assembly hall

7 in the gym

8 a fancy dress/crazy clothes

Kompetenzbereich: *Language in use*

M1 Comparisons

JIM: What's your **favourite** football team?
JACK: I think Manchester United is **the best** team in the world.
JIM: But isn't Bayern Munich **as good as** Manchester United?
JACK: I think Manchester United are even better **than** Bayern Munich because they have the **most expensive** players of all European teams.
JIM: But that doesn't always mean that they are better. Sometimes a young talented player is **cheaper** than an older player and just as good.

M2 Conversation

1 What can we do tonight?

2 I like football but I've/have never played rugby.

3 Can I come with you?

4 Is rugby more dangerous than football?

5 I don't play in a team but I often play with my friends, just for fun.

6 Last year I watched the match between Werder Bremen and Manchester United.

7 Even my sister liked it and she isn't interested in football.

8 What does your sister like (doing)?

M3 Prepositions

1 The picture shows a family **in** the child's bedroom.

2 They are looking **at** some photographs on the carpet.

3 The child is sitting **between** the parents.

4 The Dad hasn't got any shoes **on**.

5 The child's bed is **behind** the parents.

6 There's a chest of drawers on the left and there are two photos **on top of** the chest of drawers.

7 There is a basket for a baby **beside** the bed.

8 Maybe the basket is **for** the family's new baby that will be born soon.

M4 Signs

1
- a Only bicycles may go this way. ☑
- b Only bicycles won't go this way. ☐
- c Only bicycles are allowed to go this way. ☑
- d Only bicycles shouldn't go this way. ☐

2
- a You needn't smoke here. ☐
- b You don't have to smoke here. ☐
- c You can't smoke here. ☑
- d You mustn't smoke here. ☑

3
- a You need to wear a helmet. ☑
- b You could wear a helmet. ☐
- c You have to wear a helmet. ☑
- d You would wear a helmet. ☐

4 a Animals should cross the road. ☐
b Animals might cross the road. ☑
c Animals must cross the road. ☐
d Animals can cross the road. ☑

5 a You must turn off your mobile phone. ☑
b You would like to turn off your mobile phone. ☐
c You have to turn off your mobile phone. ☑
d You can turn off your mobile phone. ☐

6 a You don't have to go 30 mph or slower anymore. ☑
b You mustn't go 30 mph or slower anymore. ☐
c You don't want to go 30 mph or slower anymore. ☐
d You don't need to go 30 mph or slower anymore. ☑

M5 Verb phrases

SALLY: Hi, Tina. Where are you going?
TINA: I have to baby-sit for my aunt, I have to look **after** her two year-old daughter. She's asleep in bed at the moment and I have to be at my aunt's house before she gets **up**.
SALLY: Where do you have to get **off** the bus?
TINA: I don't know. Let's look **at** the map over there.
SALLY: What's the name of the street that you're looking **for**?
TINA: Shop Street. But I can't find it on the map. Can you find it?
SALLY: No, I can't. You better give **up** and ask the bus driver.
TINA: Good idea!

M6 Mixed grammar and vocabulary exercise

Sometimes my parents can **be** unfair!
My parents love my little sister more **than** me.
She always **gets** what she **wants**.
But as soon as she has something she **doesn't want it** anymore.
Ten minutes ago she suddenly came into the **living room**.
I was watching a film on TV there.
She **didn't like that** and **said** to my parents:
"I **don't want to watch that!** Can I watch something **else**?"
I said:
"There isn't **anything** nice on TV for small **children**."
"But we have **lots of** nice DVDs for kids", she said and began to cry.
So of course my parents helped her and now she **is watching** her stupid film.
That's so unfair!
But tomorrow I will go **swimming** with my Dad – just the two of us.

Kompetenzbereich: *Writing*

M 1 My favourite star

Lösungsvorschlag:

Dear Mrs Lenihan,

I'm big fan of Miley Cyrus. She's 19 years old and lives in the USA. I'm a big fan of her music, which is a mixture of country music and pop. I also like watching her TV series "Hannah Montana". I have all her CDs and there's a poster of her in my room.
I would really love to meet her because I think she is very nice. We could talk about how it is to be a star.
You would make me the happiest person in the world by letting me meet her.

Yours faithfully,
Andrea

M 2 Our new house

Lösungsvorschlag:

Dear Jim,

Our new house is painted white and the roof is red. There's a big garden in front of the house. There are three bedrooms on the first floor and the kitchen, the living room and the bathroom are on the ground floor. My new room is really cool: The walls are dark blue and I have put up posters of Michael Jackson on the walls. The best thing is our own big swimming pool in the garden.

Best wishes,
Alex

M 3 The lost pencil case

Lösungsvorschlag:

It's about 20 cm long and brown with stripes in different colours.
It has a zip.
There's a pencil, a ruler and a pencil-sharpener inside.
On the ruler there's a white sticker with my name on it.